PRE-K

SIGHT WORDS

Scan the QR code
on your smart phone to see
more of Mighty Kat Press'
books for kids

NEW books added regularly

PRE-K
SIGHT WORDS

Watch confidence soar as children master 40 sight words—the words most commonly encountered in any text. Children read more fluently, write with greater ease, and spell more accurately when they know these high-frequency words!

This workbook aims to develop reading and writing skills for kids while making learning fun and easy.

MIGHTY KAT
QŘÉŚŚ

Sight Words

Pre-Kindergarten – 40 words

a	here	red
and	I	run
away	in	said
big	is	see
blue	it	the
can	jump	three
come	little	to
down	look	two
find	make	up
for	me	we
funny	my	where
go	not	yellow
help	one	you
	play	

a

Read the Word	Color the Word	Trace the Word
a	a	a

Trace it

a a a a a a a a

Write it

Find and circle the word

yellow	make	a
a	up	and
find	a	come
we	where	a

and

Read the Word	Color the Word	Trace the Word
a n d	and	a n d

Trace it

a n d   a n d   a n d

Write it

Find and circle the word

play	run	for
in	red	and
and	funny	help
I	and	and

a w a y

| a w a y | a w a y | a w a y |

Trace it

a w a y   a w a y   a w a y

Write it

Find and circle the word

down	away	me
it	away	look
jump	blue	away
away	three	to

Y
o
W
o

big

Read the Word	Color the Word	Trace the Word
big	big	big

Trace it

big big big big

Write it

- -

Find and circle the word

big	not	you
big	one	big
find	said	see
here	run	bid

blue

Read the Word	Color the Word	Trace the Word
blue	blue	blue

Trace it

blue   blue   blue

Write it

- -

Find and circle the word

blue	three	blue
the	blue	go
funny	yellow	it
can	blue	you

blue

can

Read the Word	Color the Word	Trace the Word
c a n	can	c a n

Trace it

c a n   c a n   c a n   c a n

Write it

Find and circle the word

help	down	can
can	I	a
can	can	look
here	see	make

come

Read the Word	Color the Word	Trace the Word
come	come	come

Trace it

come come come

Write it

Find and circle the word

red	up	away
a	come	we
go	come	come
come	big	where

come

down

	Color the Word	Trace the Word
down	down	down

Trace it

down   down   down

Write it

- -

Find and circle the word

down	red	two
go	come	down
three	down	to
look	down	yellow

down

down

Trace the word	Trace the word	Read the word
down	down	down

trace

Trace and write the word

write

Find and circle the word

two	down	down
down	come	go
to	down	three
yellow	down	look

find

Read the Word	Color the Word	Trace the Word
find	find	find

Trace it

find find find

Write it

Find and circle the word

yellow	find	said
funny	run	find
find	two	find
up	where	see

find

for

Read the Word	Color the Word	Trace the Word
for	for	for

Trace it

for for for for

Write it

Find and circle the word

for	make	not
for	for	we
down	in	can
little	and	for

f u n n y

Read the Word	Color the Word	Trace the Word
f u n n y	funny	f u n n y

Trace it

funny funny

Write it

Find and circle the word

is	red	find
funny	funny	my
I	said	funny
not	where	funny

funny

g o

Read the Word	Color the Word	Trace the Word
g o	g o	g o

Trace it

Write it

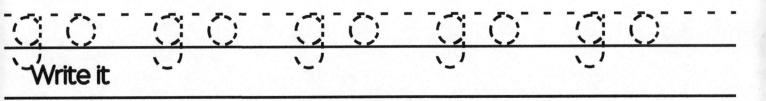

Find and circle the word

we	is	go
little	look	two
make	go	you
go	go	away

help

Read the Word	Color the Word	Trace the Word
help	help	help

Trace it

help   help   help

Write it

Find and circle the word

big	help	run
help	help	can
look	up	help
in	yellow	me

help

here

Read the Word	Color the Word	Trace the Word
here	here	here

Trace it

here here here

Write it

- - - - - - - - - - - - - - - -

Find and circle the word

red	said	here
is	see	three
blue	here	to
here	play	here

I

Read the Word	Color the Word	Trace the Word
I	0	I

Trace it

I - - - I - - - I - - - I - - - I - - - I - - - I - -

Write it

- -

Find and circle the word

I	we	down
my	funny	away
I	yellow	I
not	I	two

in

Read the Word	Color the Word	Trace the Word
in	in	in

Trace it

in in in in in

Write it

Find and circle the word

in	look	in
little	in	a
blue	in	it
we	see	come

in

Pencil Word	Color the word	Rainbow Word
in	in	in

Trace it

Stack it

Find and circle the word

in	look	in
b	in	little
ik	in	blue
come	see	we

is

Read the Word	Color the Word	Trace the Word
i s	is	i s

Trace it

i s   i s   i s   i s   i s

Write it

Find and circle the word

a	is	where
three	is	down
is	funny	jump
and	go	is

it

Read the Word	Color the Word	Trace the Word
i t	it	i t

Trace it

i t   i t   i t   i t   i t

Write it

Find and circle the word

jump	down	it
where	away	it
see	and	big
it	it	three

if

Read the Word	Color the Word	Trace the Word
if	if	if

Trace it

with

Find and circle the word

jump	down	if
where	away	if
see	and	big
if	if	three

jump

Read the Word	Color the Word	Trace the Word
j u m p	jump	j u m p

Trace it

j u m p   j u m p   j u m p

Write it

- - - - - - - - - - - - - - - -

Find and circle the word

funny	jump	not
jump	in	find
jump	where	jump
it	play	one

jump

little

Read the Word	Color the Word	Trace the Word
little	little	little

Trace it

little little little

Write it

Find and circle the word

little	little	find
a	three	up
I	come	little
me	here	little

look

Read the Word	Color the Word	Trace the Word
look	look	look

Trace it

look look look

Write it

Find and circle the word

l	we	to
look	said	look
come	funny	two
look	away	not

look

make

Read the Word	Color the Word	Trace the Word
make	make	make

Trace it

make make make

Write it

- -

Find and circle the word

big	down	where
three	play	it
two	make	make
make	make	see

make

m e

Read the Word	Color the Word	Trace the Word
m e	me	m e

Trace it

m e m e m e m e m e

Write it

- -

Find and circle the word

come	me	help
me	my	here
not	I	me
we	me	little

me

m y

<u>Read</u> the Word	<u>Color</u> the Word	<u>Trace</u> the Word
m y	my	m y

Trace it

m y   m y   m y   m y   m y

Write it

- - - - - - - - - - - - - - - - -

Find and (circle) the word

my	three	play
up	my	come
little	where	my
my	funny	is

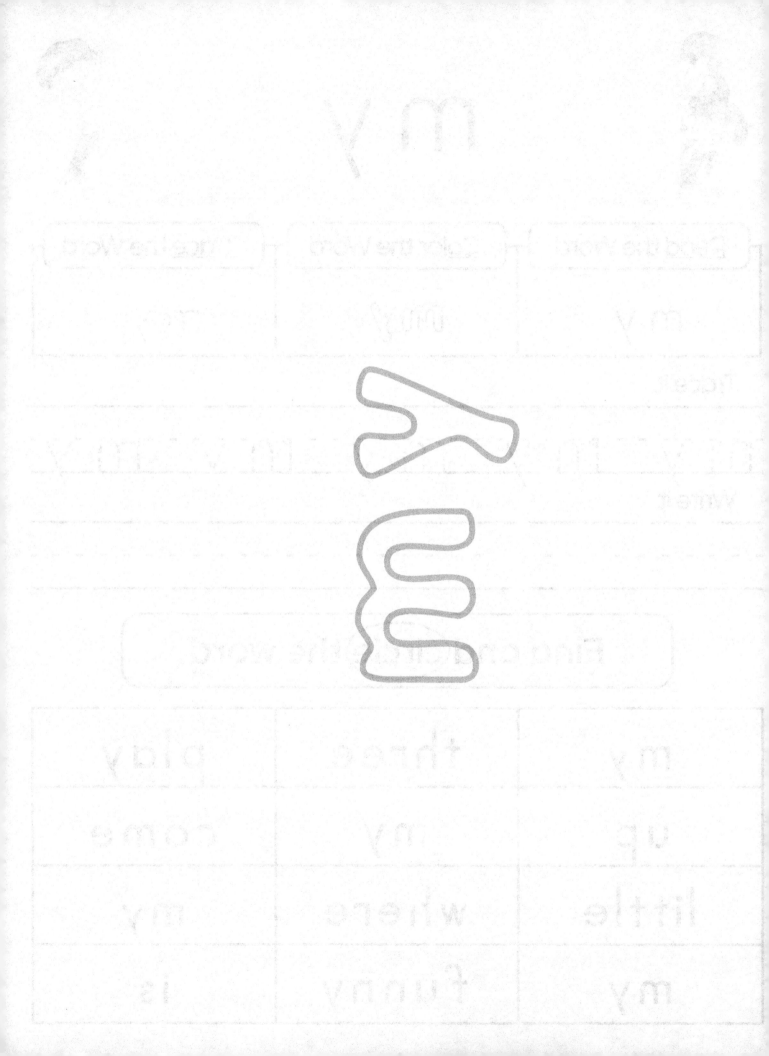

n o t

Read the Word	Color the Word	Trace the Word
n o t	n o t	n o t

Trace it

n o t   n o t   n o t   n o t

Write it

Find and circle the word

play	jump	not
not	down	two
not	in	red
come	not	look

not

one

Read the Word	Color the Word	Trace the Word
o n e	one	o n e

Trace it

one one one one

Write it

Find and circle the word

one	red	said
and	one	one
come	see	run
three	one	blue

one

one

Trace

Write it

ONE

Find and color the word

blue	red	one
one	one	and
run	see	come
three	one	blue

play

Read the Word	Color the Word	Trace the Word
play	play	play

Trace it

play play play

Write it

Find and circle the word

run	find	play
a	look	play
where	funny	here
play	play	said

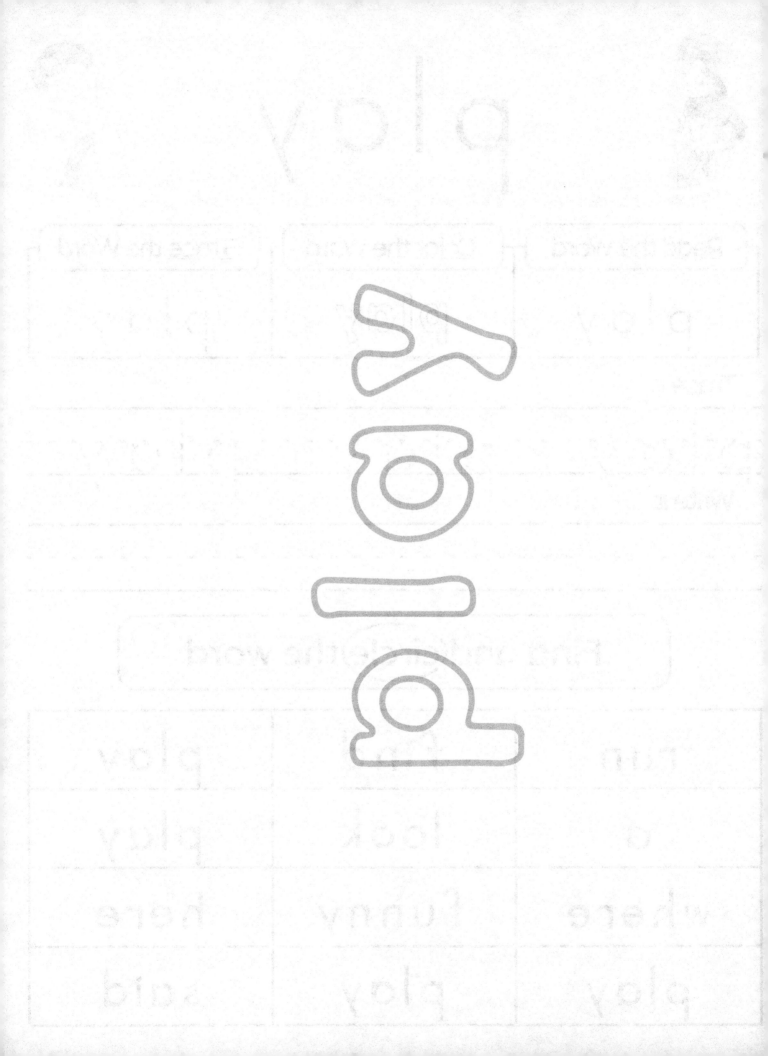

red

Read the Word	Color the Word	Trace the Word
red	red	red

Trace it

red red red red

Write it

- -

Find and circle the word

yellow	where	go
big	red	can
red	red	away
red	up	I

red

red

Read the Word	Color the Word	Trace the Word
red	red	red

Write

Find and color the word

yellow	where	go
big	red	can
red	red	away
red	up	I

run

Read the Word	Color the Word	Trace the Word
r u n	run	r u n

Trace it

r u n   r u n   r u n   r u n

Write it

- - - - - - - - - - - - - - - - - - -

Find and circle the word

run	little	where
I	go	run
run	jump	run
for	three	yellow

run

said

Read the Word	Color the Word	Trace the Word
said	said	said

Trace it

said said said

Write it

Find and circle the word

three	said	run
go	yellow	said
make	said	here
we	said	see

s e e

Read the Word	Color the Word	Trace the Word
s e e	see	s e e

Trace it

see see see see

Write it

Find and circle the word

two	look	a
see	see	see
to	in	where
red	where	see

see

the

Read the Word	Color the Word	Trace the Word
the	the	the

Trace it

the the the the the

Write it

- -

Find and (circle) the word

said	go	the
I	for	play
is	the	the
the	come	my

the

the

Read the word	Say the word	Trace the word
the	the	the

Find and color the word

the	go	said
play	for	
the	the	is
the	come	my

three

| three | three | three |

Trace it

three three three

Write it

- -

Find and circle the word

three	funny	see
three	a	red
one	three	three
here	jump	you

to

Read the Word	Color the Word	Trace the Word
to	to	to

Trace it

to   to   to   to   to

Write it

Find and circle the word

one	to	where
not	to	yellow
to	three	away
come	funny	to

to

Read the Word | Color the Word | Trace the Word
to | to | to

Find and circle the word

where	to	one
yellow	to	not
away	three	to
come	funny	to

t w o

Read the Word	Color the Word	Trace the Word
t w o	two	t w o

Trace it

t w o   t w o   t w o   t w o

Write it

Find and circle the word

not	go	it
two	said	two
look	find	two
up	two	jump

two

u p

Read the Word	Color the Word	Trace the Word
u p	up	u p

Trace it

u p   u p   u p   u p   u p

Write it

Find and circle the word

up	help	said
I	up	up
blue	down	up
red	three	up

up

Build the Word   Color the Word   Trace the Word

up   up   up

trace it

What

Find and Color the word

up	help	said
i	up	up
blue	down	up
red	three	up

we

Read the Word	Color the Word	Trace the Word
we	we	we

Trace it

we we we we we

Write it

Find and circle the word

to	down	we
yellow	look	we
run	we	you
we	funny	can

we

where

	Color the Word	Trace the Word
where	where	where

Trace it

where   where

Write it

Find and circle the word

where	you	two
is	where	three
run	funny	big
where	where	in

yellow

Read the Word	Color the Word	Trace the Word
yellow	yellow	yellow

Trace it

yellow yellow

Write it

Find and circle the word

yellow	me	three
yellow	down	for
blue	in	yellow
funny	yellow	see

you

	Color the Word	Trace the Word
y o u	you	y o u

Trace it

you you you you

Write it

- - - - - - - - - - - - - - - -

Find and circle the word

big	you	come
two	you	where
find	to	you
play	away	you

Read the Word	Color the Word	Trace the Word
you	you	you
trace		

Find and Color the Word

big	you	come
two	you	where
find	to	you
play	away	you

Color the lollipop with the word
not

SIGHT WORDS 1

n	n	o	s	o	m	p	u	q	w
f	i	n	d	s	o	e	d	r	b
e	z	u	l	t	x	r	w	f	c
c	o	m	e	t	v	a	f	k	l
p	t	n	b	c	b	w	o	g	o
i	u	n	l	a	s	a	r	w	d
l	l	t	u	n	b	y	w	x	a
a	l	a	e	d	i	u	v	k	n
l	x	h	k	s	g	q	g	n	d
o	o	g	d	o	w	n	l	s	f

a	big	come	for
and	blue	down	
away	can	find	

*** Solutions at the end of book ***

Color the sun with the word
you

Insert the missing vowel

_ n d	j _ m p
l _ t t l _	b l _ _
l _ _ k	_ t
h _ r _	p l _ _
b _ g	t h _
t w _	n _ t
f _ n d	c _ m _
w h _ r _	_ p
m _	h _ l p
_ n	_ _

SIGHT WORDS 2

e	h	o	i	t	b	i	n	j	b
l	j	u	m	p	u	e	h	f	s
o	b	h	j	m	k	r	t	i	k
o	h	e	l	p	c	j	n	l	i
k	g	r	f	u	n	n	y	u	m
x	t	e	n	z	o	o	o	b	x
s	l	i	t	t	l	e	r	d	m
l	g	o	i	v	x	q	l	a	f
u	w	l	s	c	p	u	d	l	r
o	o	w	n	o	m	m	w	l	w

funny	here	it	look
go	in	jump	
help	is	little	

*** Solutions at the end of book ***

Color the balloon with the word
away

you

away

two

jump

away

little

away

MAZE 1

in

in

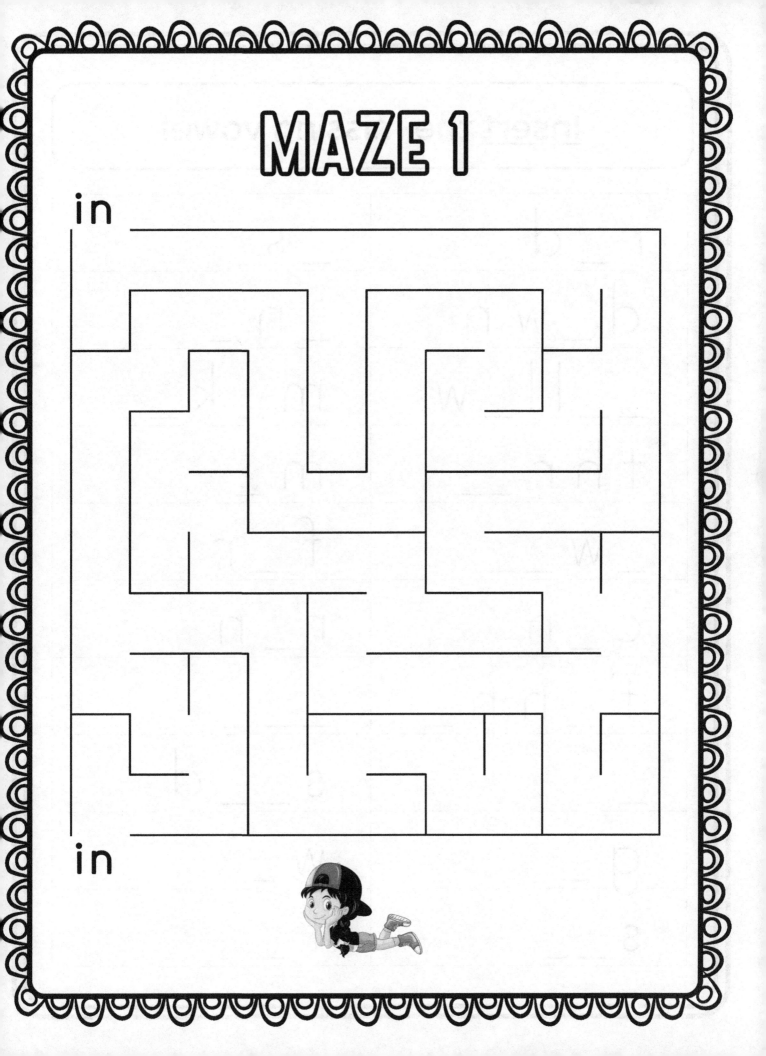

Insert the missing vowel

r _ d	_ s
d _ w n	_ n _
_ _ l l _ w	m _ k _
t h r _ _	m _
_ w _ _	f _ r
c _ n	r _ n
f _ n n _	_ _ _
_	s _ _ d
g _	w _
s _ _	t _

Color the flower with the word
two

Color the apple with the word
help

SIGHT WORDS 3

k	a	b	i	u	o	o	n	e	m
z	j	d	w	o	m	a	k	e	r
j	r	u	x	p	l	a	y	v	e
d	u	s	m	b	n	n	o	t	d
q	v	p	a	u	m	y	u	u	c
s	r	s	q	r	w	j	r	q	a
a	u	e	t	w	r	b	k	f	v
i	n	e	k	l	x	k	m	m	k
d	u	h	x	m	o	d	l	e	j
s	c	m	i	m	e	m	t	k	v

make   not   red   see

me   one   run

my   play   said

*** Solutions at the end of book ***

Color the rocket with the word
find

MAZE 2

can

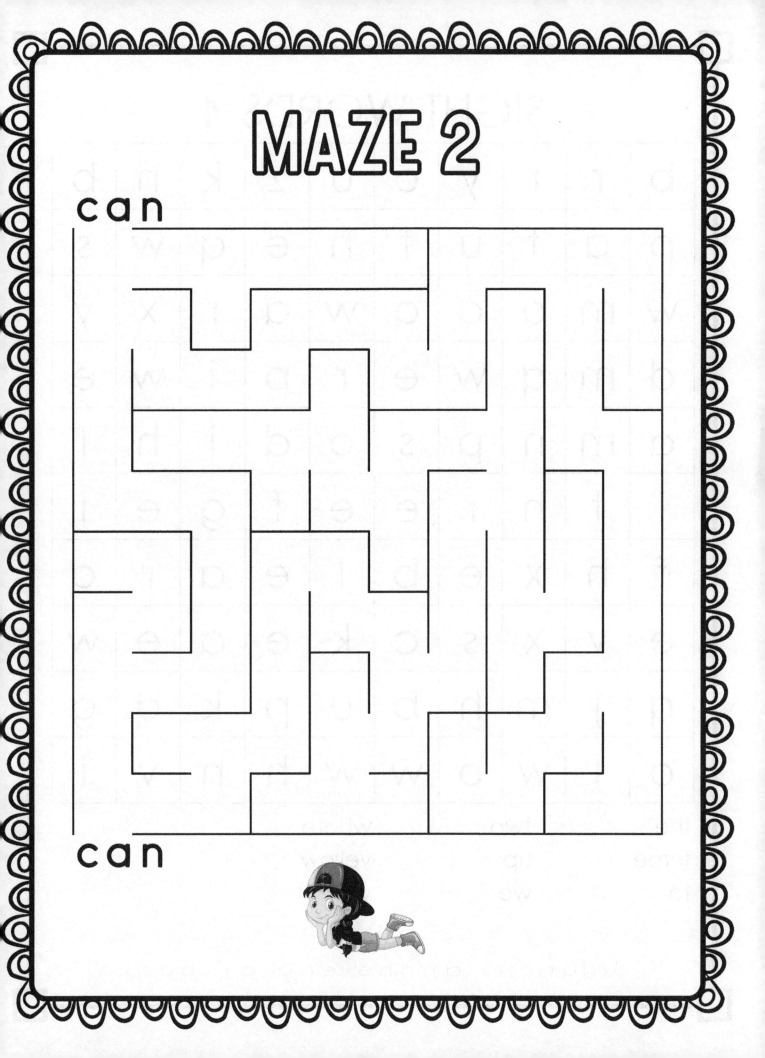

can

SIGHT WORDS 4

b	r	r	y	o	u	z	k	n	b
p	a	t	u	t	h	e	q	w	s
w	m	o	a	q	w	a	r	x	y
d	m	q	w	e	r	p	i	w	e
a	m	n	p	s	o	d	i	h	l
j	t	h	r	e	e	f	g	e	l
f	h	x	e	b	l	e	a	r	o
e	v	x	s	c	k	e	a	e	w
q	j	m	h	b	u	p	k	q	g
o	t	w	o	w	w	h	n	v	i

the	two	where
three	up	yellow
to	we	you

*** Solutions at the end of book ***

Color the cupcake with the word
red

MAZE 3

to

to

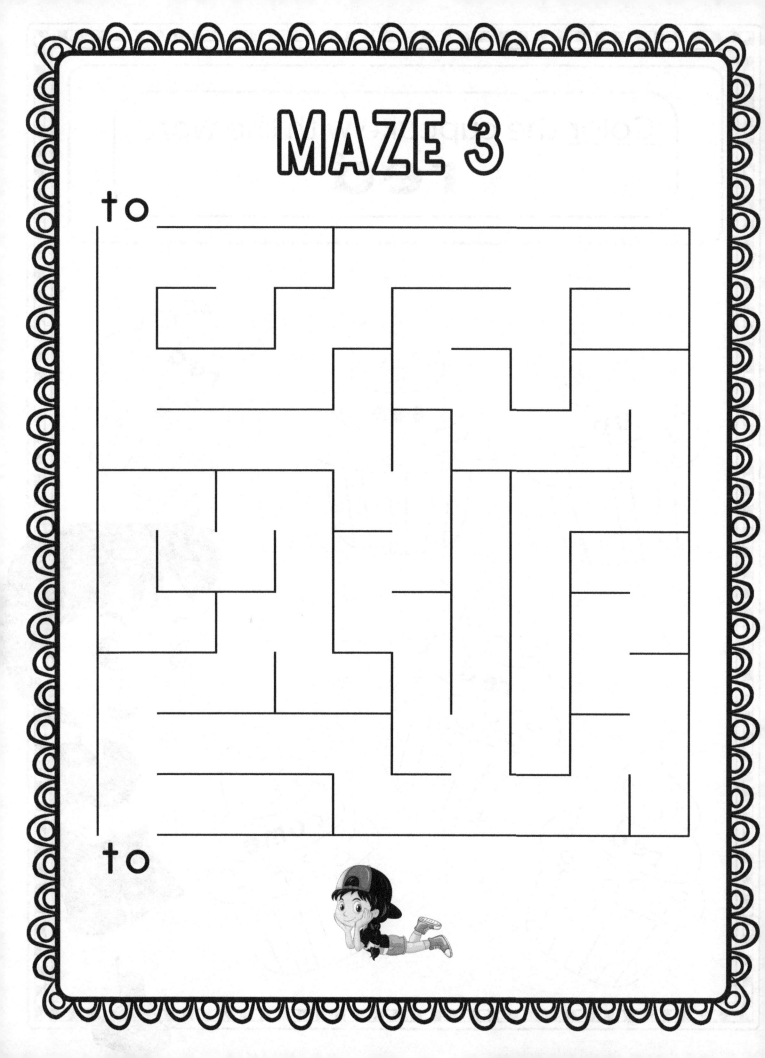

Color the pencil with the word
yellow

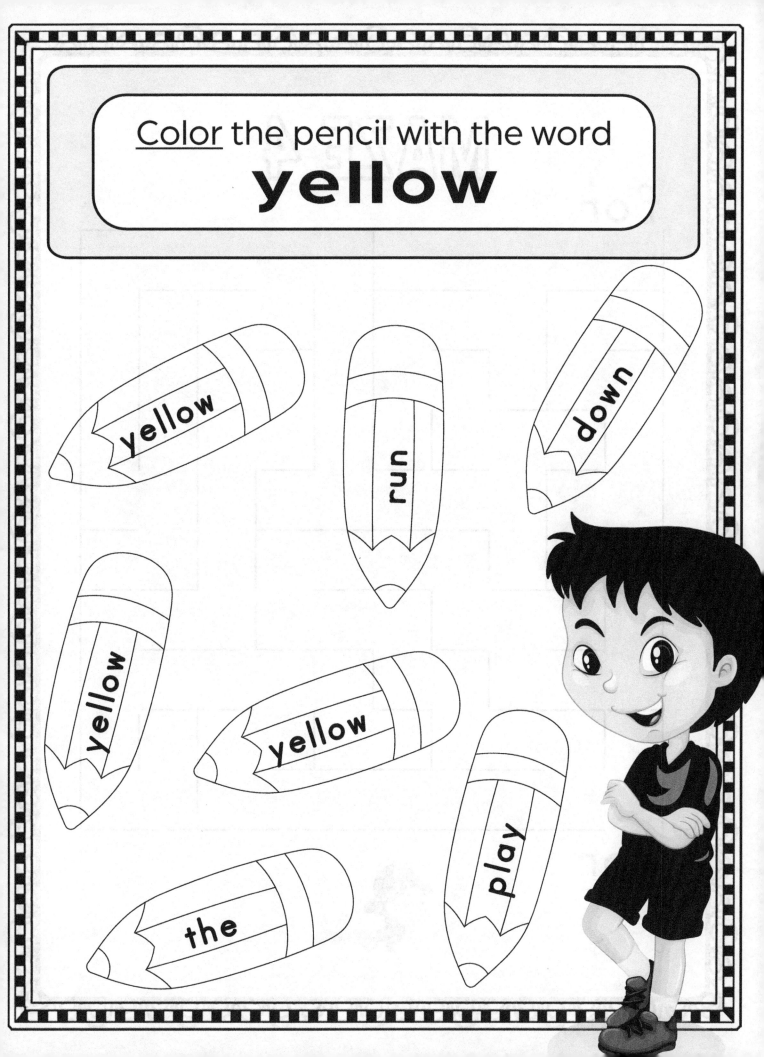

MAZE 4

for

for

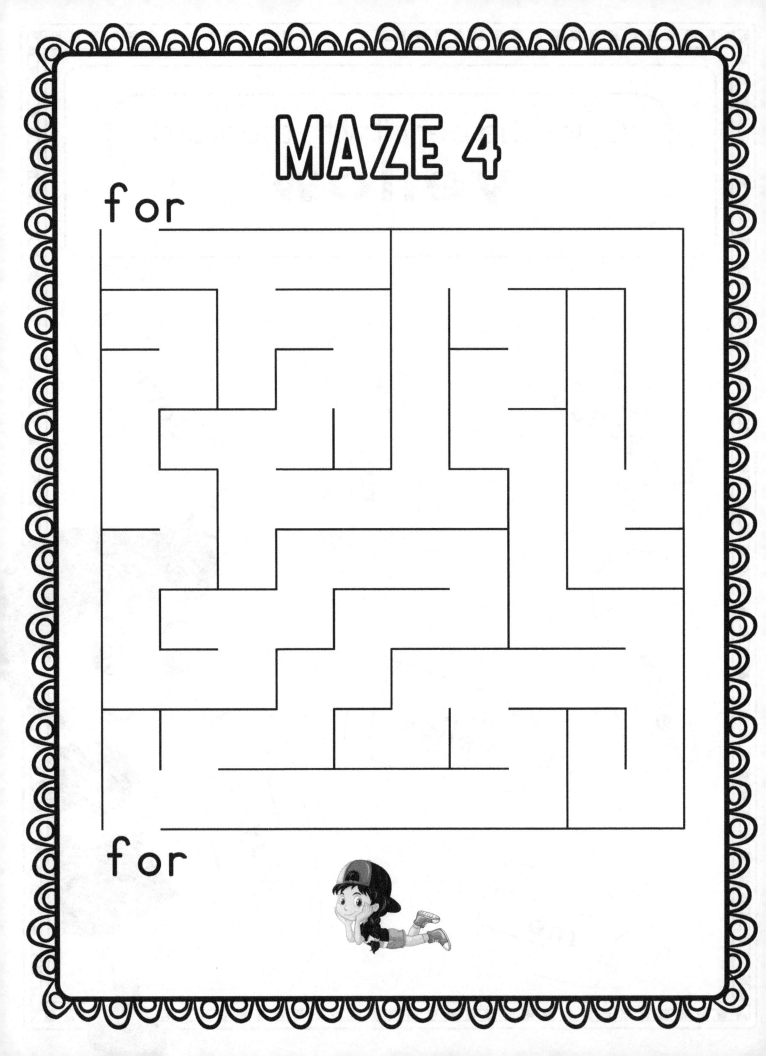

SOLUTIONS

Maze Solutions

MAZE 1

in

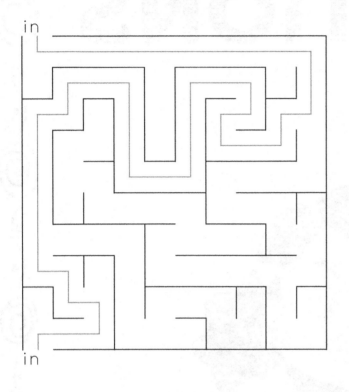

in

MAZE 2

can

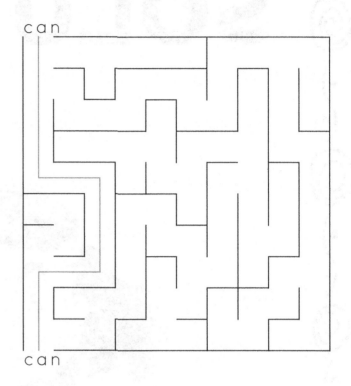

can

MAZE 3

to

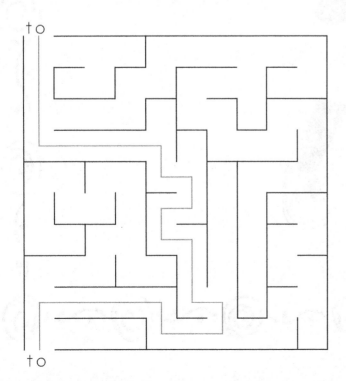

to

MAZE 4

for

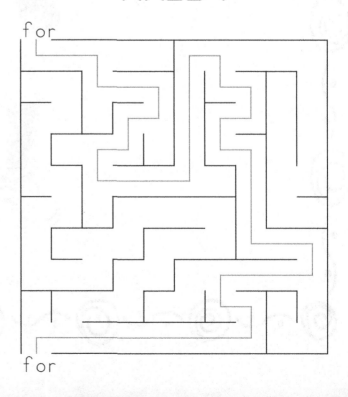

for

Word Search Solutions

SIGHT WORDS 1

f	i	n	d				
c	o	m	e		a	f	
		b	c		w	o	
		l	a		a	r	
		u	n	b	y		a
a		e		i			n
				g			d
		d	o	w	n		

a big come for
and blue down
away can find

SIGHT WORDS 2

		i	t			i	n
l	j	u	m	p			
o		h					
o		h	e	l	p		
k		r	f	u	n	n	y
		e					
		l	i	t	t	l	e
		g	o	i			
			s				

funny here it look
go in jump
help is little

SIGHT WORDS 3

				o	n	e	
			m	a	k	e	r
		p	l	a	y		e
			n	o	t	d	
			m	y			
s	r	s					
a	u	e					
i	n	e					
d							
		m	e				

make not red see
me one run said
my play

SIGHT WORDS 4

		y	o	u			
	t		t	h	e		
	o						y
		w	e			w	e
						h	l
t	h	r	e	e		e	o
						r	w
						e	w
				u	p		
t	w	o					

the two where
three up yellow
to we you

DIPLOMA

Your are on your way to becoming a reader!

has completed all the activities in

Pre-K Sight Words

GREAT JOB!

Thank You!

For your purchase

MIGHTY KAT

QŘĚŚŚ

Made in the USA
Monee, IL
21 November 2023